WITCH

PHILIP MATTHEWS

ALICE JAMES BOOKS
Farmington, Maine
alicejamesbooks.org

WITCH

10 9 8 7 6 5 4 3 2 1

Alice James Books are published by Alice James Poetry Cooperative, Inc.,
an affiliate of the University of Maine at Farmington.

Alice James Books
114 Prescott Street
Farmington, ME 04938
www.alicejamesbooks.org

Library of Congress Cataloging-in-Publication Data

Names: Matthews, Philip, 1987– author.
Title: Witch / Philip Matthews.
Description: Farmington : Alice James Books, 2020
Identifiers: LCCN 2019036026 (print) | LCCN 2019036027 (ebook)
   ISBN 9781948579087 (paperback) | ISBN 9781948579643 (ebook)
Subjects: LCGFT: Poetry.
Classification: LCC PS3613.A8495 W58 2020 (print) | LCC PS3613.A8495 (ebook)
   DDC 811/.6—dc23
LC record available at https://lccn.loc.gov/2019036026
LC ebook record available at https://lccn.loc.gov/2019036027

Alice James Books gratefully acknowledges support from individual donors, private
foundations, the University of Maine at Farmington, the National Endowment for the
Arts, and the Amazon Literary Partnership.

Cover art: Carly Ann Faye

CONTENTS

For francine j. harris, Jagdeep Raina,
JE Baker, and Sam Ross
for their generosity with this work

Each chakra described with a different number of petals

pédale; pédé: faggot

DECIDUOUS

The priests went away nodding
that an amputated arm was a failure,
circumambulating
an intense interior. They became

a murmuring woods,
desperate for light, tearing
their breasts like hydrangeas, a second
shed on the floor of needles.

The priests went away nodding
that an amputated arm was a failure.

Asked her for her claw and whisky.

Bit down on a branch.

Said the patient to the fire, "I'm all
swaddled up in my shit, and sad.

What can you tell me
of disappearing?"

Lightning.

"And seed?"

Tree; it fears the colonizer.

WHAT RAN BRIGHTNESS

She wants me to weep.
She wants to marry me
if I am patient, wild enough.
Folded into my calm like a pattern
I would wear. What ran brightness
rubbed down to rock
I keep buried just inside
my breastbone. I know

that for a moment, our fingertips pressed, my middle finger
pressed, I sent a message
I had thrown up a scrim, a boundary
that would protect us
both,
and for a time, I could stay flaccid,
until two
wildernesses came over me.
I had *reason* to fear

as heaven hatched:
this was the beginning of Petal,
sometimes.

Sometimes she is a self-formed being,
ouroboric river.
Sometimes she is a friend or a mother

in an apple-print dress,
holding my hand, leading us, hermit-like,
through the forest.
Until upon a house we spot, we
weeding and bramble
upon and crack the whole thing
in and crush it. Ivy in the trundle bed,
locusts in the seams.
Moping over dishes, inhabitants
and cream. Inhabitants
bathing with a teacup of water,
one each. As off across a sticky
cloud, attempts three times to break in, one
eye kept on the doorknob.

Petal has changed since the green
stone was plowed up with the harvest—
obsequious—slightly opaque weight except
in moonlight, direct
beam to ghostly liver. All day she sweats,
her face flushed, her hands loose from storage
angle to my breasts, my throats, and I
like it. Don't I own her throat, too?
I rinse her cock with
abundant energy. Long times I
watch her from the punch spirit forward,
re-tin the barnside, cut the copper.
To tell her / if they are nearby. She is as if
electrocuted with ghosts, beating at the stone
at her throat, shower of glass.

PERHAPS THERE'S SOMETHING IN THIS BAG FOR YOU

A shaken calf or Calvinist
unhooked from his bones, such a pretty
        structure and slim; or an empty
dreaming
        boarhound.
Our family argues with the
        witch . . . *Is she a man: Petal? OK, she's a man;*
is she a woman: Petal? OK, she's a woman . . .
        as we use the broccoli-stalk
wand to break four copper basins on a
        wooden altar:
blood, honey, vinegar, water
        pour out at various speeds,
or not at all, depending on
        where we struck and the level
each basin was filled;
        we are trying
to scry out
        a gender. The witch is telling us
where we can go, calling out the name of God, a curse
        on our heads and our house, a name
she could only know if God has told it
        to her like God has told it to me;
I break off the limp
        parts of the wand and throw them
into hydrangea bushes

*

... wake
      in a bed full of dried hydrangeas,
oak pods (?), and hiding brown recluses
      towards the feet, the hydrangea
bush and oak tree growing bedside,
half my body uncovered / unwound
from the pulled duvet / desert,
the sun shining weakly in.

Petal, perhaps you might tell me, in a
word, what you want;
      ... *lovers, spleens, baskets* ...
That's three words, Petal, three
      good words, we can do that.
And once we've been accomplished,
      you might move your claw off
      my lap, I am
asking nicely. There will be no need
for a tantrum here. We've been
discussing, for a long time now,
what happened in the Christmas tree lot:

*

Demure, you knelt in your
      headscarf to touch them, their
sappy spines / trunks, readied for

a sticking-in, ready
for a living room carol, father
off-key, grandmother
drinking whisky from a golden flask / flash.
Petal, what did they tell you
about death and arrangement,
adornment that's made you so
angry? I
can't place a comb in your
hair without you cringing: *You*
cringing, I'm fine. I could take
all combs from this fireplace
right now. And yet,
we can't shake the memory of the
guard patrolling the pen,
keeping the Christmas trees in.
His cuff links in straight starlight and
freezing.

*

Petal, covered in frost with your sisters,
evergreen, evergreen, fanning out
and being climbed by spiders whose
webs you wore to the fairgrounds;
turning your bushel and branches
to the most fitting light as the
barker called your number,
your siblings shivering bundles
behind you,

waiting or having had
their turn. In the audience, two women measured
        your frame with a cut of their
hands and one
        bled all over the snow. You know
how little it *seems* to take
        to be pleasing / pleasuring / something you could do
with your eyes off / without being
        removed. Elsewhere, the Ferris wheel
rolled like a wrist, bedecked with
        paws and ropes.

PETAL CAME TUMBLING, TUMBLING

It was 1916.

I floated out past the icebergs, a shadow of a blue whale underneath,
  almost a ship in the sense that one might stand on it riskily. From
  the other side: blue / smoke / angels

and me not in on

a bad joke. I built my own

chapel of moss and hard

mollusks / and crowned my neck

with heavy jewels. Black at the Adam's apple

where I wished to suck out an oval.

Orbitly I came ashore.

Orbitly I walked for days, pocking for shelter

around the vine,

around the red bird's foot,

around the starfish fossil and calling out for my father or mother,

sleeping on my feet as weary as new rice.

I heard the witch's name

on a stone, weather-beaten,

washed out almost

to the point of mythology:

a small boy

placing hands / at the bedsheet,

and daring to see

his father, pulled back,

tidal in the halo

just outside the window: his face

muscles sink and almost,

for a slick second, are whalebone;
in other words, expensive.
Silver. Aluminum.
Silver.

TAROT

At sunrise, the angels arrive
with their diet of crabs and clams
to crash against the breakwater.
Hundreds shatter, are taken
behind the frenzy, and after—
the divining pools of shellwater,
shells of broken fire, violet
and white,
wet feathers, red legs,
birdshit.
I take my mother

as a memory down
this bridge, surefooted
with healthy knees, joints
shifting in their tissue as they should.
There is a vision
in which seven legs
relate to each other on rock—
There will be a book,
but no grandchildren.
There will be a husband
like four birds low
over earth. There will be a skin
to be in, sword pulled
from a crane's heart, sack of meat.
As my mother is vertical

on seawater.
And now kneeling.

We have been talking about prophecy,
the delicate balance
of inhabiting somebody's consciousness,
fire in a glass.
One holds the other down
to her chair, saying,
Don't get up.
There is work here, the floor
of the sandswept room to be swept,
glass doors open
to the seaside. The access of lit wind
consistently.
Mother in her robe of white
daggers, tending the curtains,
smoothing the bed, unhooking
the neck of the crane.
This is a gift. This is to be
a gift.

THE TRANNY BALLET

A petal was a *shing* mirror.

A petal watched a leap.

I walked into that light and the audience

were bacterial, set against a cloudy sky,

only partly mine.

I came to a point I did not feel supported

by my role: like trying to balance on a branch

blown vertical

and simultaneously apologizing for my phallus.

The set was burning. I brought my hoof closer to my sister's face,

(we were playing the role of siblings) and turned her ember eye

to the skylight.

There was the claw. There was the cross-thrush

of branches / quilt / scratch marks.

I bent / around / my sister,

gazing towards an orbit and following. The audience

were too much to think about, I thought, and turned my attention

to smaller flashes:

a leaf's light on a costume, a stole line

of thread, a silken hoof and the girl attached to it,

pushing me away. The room

was split into: mine, "hers," and the audience

delicately arranging their feet. Turning was a vertical feat,

and what a shamble

to mistakenly drop the rock from my head

and silently signal my sister to return it.

Mountain-hard water.

Kiss: a rolling bloom.

        These
were instructions I repeated to myself
to get through the sex scene.

I attempted to keep my posture,

but my feet were shining mirrors:

alit a rock,

alit a wig and bramble,

alit a thorn's puncture, alit a face

tuned to television,

alit a woman's hand, girl with

rabbit's claw, dancing the swan

wings, out-retched and soiled, the blindfolded

head and sink-enk,

avoiding an ax.

Then the upswing was as a swung

mirror, the

audience tangled in white.

. . . splinter

awareness

sound

ebbed

the waves of a cracked branch . . .

Slowly each rough face feathered,
and flickered over the blue eggs; water
like a mattress filled in
to a certain height. There were four
nests in the water,
four goose heads,
satellites to a core

which was the
rubbed body flesh each

head wanted. My body
quaked inside the water like a live oak

; I called into my neck for
vocal cords, finding none

THE FIVE SHADES IN HER NECK

Petal peels back you.
Bell stitched to her headskin.
Bicycle.
Chased through the eighth sun.
She freezes.
She is a strict gun.
Stunning you with her hand.
Her hand immediately in your hair.
Puny Red.   (Here we hear Petal. The neck turns left *Puny*
then

                       right Red. But we do not hear her correctly. We
                       hear what we want / said, *Roomy red,* running
                       our hand through our wound.)
Tined and constellated.
The targeting wind in her neck.

THE PRIEST AND WARRIOR

Priest who washes the blood from my
        breast . . . dove's wing
cloth
        that peels a residue
of necessary trauma
        from sunlit skin and
eye at his lip whom
        Apollo blesses.
Apollo's keen collarbone
        installed
in him . . .
        where I place my temple
and wait for his hand

        to fall down . . .
pentecostal,
        epileptic,
birdlike . . . strobic
        ride in the pine needles,
tipped tar.
        What oracle droning
through his open mouth and my
        tongue
receiving. Violet gown
        thrown

to the statue's feet. The flower-streaks
        there, tubes thrashed

in the night wind, veins like
         full-burst lilacs,
kicking,
         against slack
blooms impressed
         like hanging mouths . . .

*

On this copper ground: heads bent
         to wind . . . honeybee
doing its work from space
         to space where the violet socket
eyes glow and
         the violet light cupping
in softened palms. Where ants like
         onyx powder . . . crystallized . . .
might drink
         that sugar unto
coalesced, concentrated. Should I
         ask the mind
to be strict in its gaze . . .
         film of easy storm
over ocean and
         whale glimmer
like flame in a bull's skull
         behind
giant wave . . . I should ask
         what bigness is for when
ground down

into copper dust. How attached
to each particle then
I am.
Wafer
of copper sun arc.

THE MORNING STAR

Satan turns on his wheel of light,
hovering inside the Senate.

A beauty confesses to the power of air,
a roaring socket of need.

The humans bear forth from their jelly,
six rose-lipped mannequins.

—Who among these is most loved?

We will be forthright in our character analysis.
We will stenograph on bright, bright branches.

Even as someone might bribe us:
with a basket of fruit to our hearth;

with a length of black thread to our dead;
with a boy with that thread in his heart;

with a boy with a snail in his heart;
with a boy with toys in his heart, who are bowing.

A NEW FUNCTION

My mind is not quiet. Voices warble
from behind the plaster walls as if from underwater.
My lover gives me his usual look of confusion.
It is not his emergency. He does not even notice
the noise until I mention it, superior as he is.
On good days, he binds me in his legs.
Shut in, it is possible to tolerate the neighbors.
Otherwise, the voices are not human behind the walls
the idea of black widows stalks across. Such rage
passes through me. I have begun to think
it is my natural being, like a stone set mysteriously
in an empty field. I have forgotten everything else,
though I am a thriving colony where I am,
distant from rational worldview. It is almost spring.

We have gone outdoors for quiet, with the purple
snow-hat blooms, the umbrella's regular static
above us. Our boots are traction-steady, and stoned,
the world is bright: no guests, just the two of us out
with the full or not full houses, the curb
where someone has left a kitchen sink. It has filled
with snow as adequately as a water glass
or a mirror might.

HOW GRIEF IS INSCRIBED IN A LOVER'S INTESTINAL LINING

Violet tissue, compressed gold duodenum
where the "holy ghost" lives, the site of optimum iron absorption
in mammals. In the cow's four-part stomach,
I lay down my head and
am patient, for what? the moon's shroud
to cover it, clear it, and something new to crystallize,
just wet. In the twelfth house, a demon roars in the dark,
ten to twelve feet tall.
Like what is Petal's house

in the cow's stomach?
Kind of like Snow White's:
tin dishes, a wooden table, a trundle to sleep in,
a selenite egg to hold memory, fear, and surpass nouns,
onyx knives, onyx forks, silver spoons, the chicken tasting of metal,
even living,
mutual bonds neatly in a row, she blesses their foreheads
each night, tin pot, leaking roof, a river in the lining,
a jar of jelly and a jellyfish,
a yellow chair, so cruelly broken.

While the cow is couched
in a pine forest, small, black thing.

HOUSEGUEST

If you were Satan, you'd be pissed too, asked to kneel

before God made flesh, not even, the prototype of God made flesh,
the practice round, idiot man stumbling through the garden, God's
legs

keeping him upright. Then came the woman with an actual brain,
who is closer to the idea God has. Let's call her Petal, who reaches
her

claw to the thin-skinned fruit that, in picking, finds her her hand,
in eating, finds her two lips like two rosebuds that can

speak, rub and vibrate, pop and ring aloud as well as in her head,
in contract with the garden snake, finds her her twice-threaded
DNA, both godly and human, which was

God's idea in the first place, God in the first place. At
Christmastime, the Christians bring

the tiny breads to their mouths. I carol along with them, even I
have a sun-god to celebrate the coming of, the solstice pushing
back the winter's night

like an eroding shoreline, Satan's wing tip picking up slack earth,
until black as the land he is working in, he brings forth
wheat fields to feed us, in daylight, firelight, shepherds

dozing among them, more vigilant at night. I can almost see the
raised scythe. I wonder what my mother, ordained, is thinking

as she shares the fire in her hand with me, who was born again
and now is not, pagan in a sheep's wool, taking the sheep's breast
in my mouth, as twelve

deacons, all men, stand ominous in candle-shadow before us.

WOODEN CRADLE IN THE WOODS AND VISITORS

To come into the dark voice of fire Algae
rain, clipped
telephone line fizzing Communicating
by distant light
the last texts of being alive
Papaya coil, roll my head in it

Whoever crosses—in robes, antler-crowns—rock, black and bulbous—
for something hidden—through algae rain

Opening an eye, a snail in the socket in the woods

A wooden cradle also in the woods

*

Visitor: To acknowledge an emptiness, observed in time (observed
reluctance   splitting off)

        To participate   (forked /
under the sky,   constellated
                                        at the throat, who
and then, under the rock sky we carry,   is
        each of us feeling an I

                blue ridge, the deer's /   making it
                                move to her behaviors
                                and wishes)

Feet on our back ribs, migrating, this year,
without us

In hunching under the
westward storm

                                Visitor: I can't
know exactly who is there in the house one
star lights above,
an obfuscation moved slightly but—for better /
which is to say more clarified / clear—
light

Going while
        the photographer
positions my body
        within a frame—rosemary and cat.

rosemary and pine without light.
rosemary and pinned structure.

Thor in my side of pennied / penned-in water, cow
bathing in the flooded yard. mind
                              with thought

or mind in an emptiness whirling /
were-ing / wearing a dress.
            arms struggling to get out of
                  arms

Visitor: Where he churched, king's angel carries teeth

MADE TO ALWAYS WORSHIP AT
ONE STATION

After Bernini

Headless angel kneeling, mark of the
hand at his back;
headless angel showing off,
headless angel showing off;

—That's the first thing. Then the envisioner, a poet a king who is
hunting. We must be in an earlier time, with kings on horseback or
foot, at night they do what they want. Somewhere kings can be poets
or hunters or a very graceful prophet once in awhile. So this:

The envisioner enshrouded by forest darkness
from which light, atrophied, appears—wings tangled in a branch-
	system;
torso set on a stump and reeled out, tightening
the distance between bear bait and catcher; the envisioner
still in his pod

as around him the night packs, the night birds, the night snakes and
	night fish,
the night insects, charged from their sockets, emerge, accomplish
their small, vital works, the angels
extending their heads to listen; the envisioner, by lantern

*

gives willingly to the trees ninety bodies,
feels the shell of his militancy growing, hard
at his shoulders and navel, stones at his crotch
and heels; feels into the space of his lover's
hard-on, heart salved
then split; the thicket of his spit through which voice
comes, amalgamous and sudden
as theatre; a flesh

*

wills a king to place upon a dish its heart
and start towards the forest in blindness, to sing
in the dead of winter's night, splintered from the deep
nails down into the reins
of charity's first thunderous mainship these
horrid songs without thought, comforting
to the heart in its rage; to cross a river,

lifting the trayed heart overhead, the king half-drowning
in the effort, as overhead the vultures sweat
patiently by; the envisioner

*

hunched under the full light of heaven—disfigured brethren
with ten thousand arms, covered in eyes and their lashes; caged

is the last human thought; caged is the paw
on its pine-straw floor.

*

"I do not think to be crucified, though it is meant for me.
My vision is wasted on this wreckage-sight, spilled.
My mother is patient and grieving; a great trust
crosses between us

when I decide to die, undo what she has given over to protecting
until now: my perishable body. The angels
in their snail-pods whisper, *home*, and *legislate*, they reverberate
across heaven's marble—the world's only curiosity store."

OBEDIENCE AND POSSESSION

The angels drift along the periphery
of sheep—shift with wind,
slow as real honey, slow as pulled
wool, gaze turned always
towards banishment.

The angels are still in their pods.
They will not hatch the pelicans
installed in their breasts.
They will not share their liver and heart.

JESUS

Sot, froth, I came
to know myself as a blur
in the mirror at mother's
dresser: you have not
met my mother but she is
the root plane at which I
and you
plant our face, smelling
of earth, shit, and wet
tumultuous grass, thunder
at the roots as ants and more
molecular shells
traverse their pheromonic
logic. In the creases
of mother's hands, unread
by anyone superior to her:
you may have
seen me in my seagauze
dressings spinning
quietly at the threshold
of woman, posturing
towards woman, and failing,
my work boots a dead
giveaway.

—No—I forgot—you met my mother once
as I took her down

a bridge, as a memory, but this was me
pretending I had a moment of
power.

WICCA

Mind
—bone past my wrist in its length
I have oiled
and anointed like a desert priest;

combed it with my grandmother's comb,
known kinship as if with a grantor
who might, in all likelihood, fund me
with an oracular voice—

ORACULAR, OCULAR

—Where is it written, what I will say?

—The angel's shoulders, great wheels of light
churn, visible
to Lilith's descendants, bright monsters,
mutable
bodies of water and creaturedom. Stretch
fibrous tentacles of women. An eye swims

across the horizon, a whale herd
lifting their jaws, grey
scalene apparatuses. The entirety
of their weight will drag back, the way we
cannot resist
the femur's weight. One wheel of light

is breaking, from within, a voice calling over
the sea, a voice of greed and envy
we will elect or will not elect
to heed. One wheel of light encloses
an ascetic absence.

A SUBSTITUTE

Oxygenated angels
enclosed in their mossy tubs, feathers
combed and oiled at strange angles. No one
is flying with these wings.

The angels sit in their breasts, attached
to lungs and a sleeping machine;

periodically are checked on by gloved hands
descending from the tidewater blackness;

—touching the forehead,
touching the wing joints,
touching the mouth,
touching the chest,
touching the throat,
touching the pelvis,
touching the knees,
touching the breath,
touching the spit on the earth,
in which the heart will rot, rest, wretched,
or spill.

ELECTION DAY

—Then again, there is the squabbling
leashed meat in Aisle 6, roaring its bloody
soft gums. How it does prowl
in its Styrofoam tray. How it does sleep in the light.
Before the hands swept in, before even the employees,
I was here, having slept on the floor, pouring prayers
to the cutlets and priest-joints. How it does protect itself
against the primacy of money. I am swaying my arms.
I am praising and praising and praising
as the carts roll by my martyr. How it does sniff at the herbs
in its former life it ate for itself. How it does shine
through its cover, wet ruby.

JESUS

Sunlight flickering
in the rocks at low
tide is what the drones always
wanted to be; a show
distracting
from this fascist regime.
I am thirty, and lost.
Anyway, what would it mean
to feel secure here, in the current
upon the back
of my neighbor, shuttled
to the border, and ejected?
The gull who is still on
the beach, a handsome gull,
yogic, warrior-like, thick, shifting
eye like a guard against
charlatans, shining towers some ones
could disappear into. What does it do
to grow into a role that
would kill me, effectively?
I have walked,
been walked,
to the shallow water to drown,
peered, Narcissus, in:
a candle
and a salty pine growing, illusion
from the crown of my head.

CROWN AND CROWNING

I

Fatty wind I walk into, hand
Over my belly. As the cattle inside me move.
I give it a name. Tongue resting outside of its owner.
My brain like opening to rainfall. Pine branch twist.
Gristle root. What could be inherited I curb,
Ancestral grief at the wrist I encircle with copper.
Violet light panned from beneath this skull's root.
What winds between the vertebrae
Forming in my belly. Hooves floating, waiting
To snap to the earth. Belly held over the swan's
Neck, pathetic and strong, from which I extend
A foot, a leg, a garter and voice
Expansive across the shoreline. Sister birds cut
Into the water. Cyclical shell. Dirty, flung flute.

2

Shell and flute. Shell and glimpse into the oracle
Of grieving, slick hands silver at the water bowl's
Rim. Body that is mine, raving, epileptic
Through lightning-thumped branches. At sea, in it,
I am cutting two lungs with my legs, if I think
About the sea the way the ancients did. I do.
I cock a river, discharge tidelight
Like a girl left holding the crack-bag.
Underneath me, a lilac is speaking,
Split off at the tendril from sunlight,
Thick, written tendril from chest, unfurled into the world's
Six griefs. I yank back the dog wanting to run.
My son digs for crabs at his shins, inside me,
Uncovered from a crystalline shell.

3

Soft fire, photographer, uncovered from the crystalline shell.
Dirty sheep
Backing haunches into green light of hills
Before storming. And are we permitted to be here?
As the sky comes plummeting under,
Violent rain, and the grass throwing up
Spiked energy. In the bank of the crystalline ship.
In the wrong of the crystalline place, eyes squinting,
Gamey, spun out, in orbit,
Bashing into each other's wood sides. We, like fists, do this,
Dust knotted up in our knuckles.
Here is the mason. Here is the honed wave's
Crest. Here is the black-eyed boy, name
Written in wood. Again. Again. Like we are married to it.

4

I am married to two angels, one conquered
In the ashpit, elbows shined, two small ships
Of blood. And the audience set at the glass doors
Pushing in limelight to see.
I walk away quickly. I see the slight
Where witness is buried,
And a lilac tree grows from the ashes.
For decades. There from the muck of me,
My son's liver / wishes / livery
Dangling like carrots. The little meats of him,
Costumed and sent out for silvering. I hated /
Watched him then. I could feel him
Under every cell of my skin,
Knees wedged in like a table.

5

Knees wedged in like a table. The altar
Is set to eat. I will serve you
As my father served me.
A stream of requests on your behalf:
For schools, for nannies, for chefs,
For a woman with a crooked eye I will make you call
Grandmother, for petty, pretty things,
And I will keep my hand close
To your scalpel. I mean: *skull*, photographer. Cupped.
It will be days before I look at you again.
For all you are, you could be a dingy carton of eggs
In your bedclothes, in your day clothes,
Fizzing quietly. I admire the nurses' knuckles
When they bring you in. Strange, stripped suns.

6

Strange, stippled sun, a fist of white petals.
A school. A nanny. A question. A turtle fit to bursting
Like a slowly unfurling hydrangea. I study its back
Like a menu, lifting the tendrils of creek. Small water,
Big water, what I say about the sea's push
Of climate, oil spill spreading like a lung
To the place the throat will feather,
And something, eagle-headed, sprung,
Thrusts hands into the small sprouts that feed us.
Holding open a cancerous alley, brain
Of an upset shock. The surface of a mussel-green
Molly fossil. And money and memory
Embedded in a single money's belly.
Voices a double surface from underneath which:

7

(Godly)   A voice bellows over the bath.
A mechanic nanny gives instructions
From a silver disk. I am meant to lay my son in like this, turtle shell
Wrapped in myrrh-sheets, mouth empty of water.
Contract laid between us
We are aware of as we sit down to breakfast. His limbs
Begin to grow, I hold him out. His limbs
Begin to shrink, I bathe him. It is a program
For which I am made, from which I am made
For this meat. He cries and he dreams
And is chastened. Five swords are plunged
Through his heart. He will pull a plan from his heart.
He will pull a cradle from his gut.
He will pull a servant from his head.

8

If Athena were to say back to the head,
I'm freer than I have been, in a wave
Of father's pain, farther from the shoreline (torture)
Of insight and precision, the head would listen.
Off across the way, a tithing (galaxy)
Whose gulls dive for silver sine-lines of fish
Arcing their hooked bellies to glinting. (Gills)
Like false teeth. From over the boat's edge,
Many hands reach in, pull in
The net like a father's weight. Farther off,
Forearms, and the peeling back of knives against ice beds,
Noonlight burning the shack. Who press (down)
Thin mirrors to the walls and watch
The fish heads being piled up like weights, nickel-like.

9

My figure held to nickellight,
If I look right at the camera, photographer,
Blown open reflecting white orbs
And the confident orbit of plenty,
As even at my poorest, I am bushel-brained,
Every fiber translucent and yellow,
As even at a distance, I am outlined in gold
Like the dream of a lightning-struck house,
A shock of plant life and downpour,
A world red and expensive, placed credit
To my forehead, pressed forehead
To machines, streamed brain like a river to rainfall:
I will fly. I will eat and be touched.
I will my match my name up with yours.

10

What will he do with my fingertips?
What will he do with my face?
All around me I am seeing, I am.
Off my perineum as the light will catch it,
I pluck a rooster, pick a finger.
(Godly) A voice bellows over the bath.
I lay down white petals and breasts.
I lay my hands and face at his feet
If according to this king's will.
His fibrous ribs. He is also, easily, killed,
Extended to grut. In bowls of bled water,
With a pimple at his breast-wing, thimbled leg.
I am married to two angels, one flying forward.
I will match my name up with his.

11

All around the house my son is seeing
Lines of girls in Sunday dresses with dirty stockings and shoes.
They are putting candy in his mouth.
They are coming in with metal tools,
Overlarge for their branches.
And what are they pinning now in his hands
That he is screaming starry-murder. I am not right with it.
For something to do, I rearrange the lights
On the table (utensils). I am not watching
When my son dies. Light in the roots. Light in the fire.
Light in the charred bird's beak. Light in the limestone.
Light underwater. Light in the diamond's ankh knuckle.
Compressed gold light in betrayal's long decision.
Light in the drug-in plinth.

12

Light the plinth.
It is not easy to be married to god,
Goes the servant's whistle, goes the feral pre-form, too,
Of the shepherd. There have been plenty of people
Who have drowned in the desert, pulling down thought
To try to say something. To prophet a shroud.
This man with no ribs, talking down from a plank
Of carpenter's wood. *Sweet grief,* exclaimed
As if by Southern women. I might take their voice
(Siren-like) in my throat. And the shit I would say then.
A tidy, violet light charring through.
A passed-on, stupendous root. My son
Equates bigness with price,
Something I probably taught him.

13

Photographer, I will teach you this
Absorption of shock. Stand back. As monies go,
We are doomed, doomed, politicians
Polluting the tithe waters. I watch my son
Descend the baptismal plank. His grandmother
Crying, rat-like, and I shivering in my seat
Like a rosebud. The six elders
Float above our heads with their swords.
Where can I put my eyes
That the church will not take them? The last of my money
Crouches in my purse like a death.
They will not have my lipstick.
They will not have my carousel.
They will not have my son's great foray.

14

They will not have my pregnancy in their hands.
Photographer, I will slat them where they go.
All the preachers ruffling their feathers
Can burn there. I am hot in this rage where I have been
Transformed. Do you see me with these knives
In my pupils, my hands, my heels?
Perhaps they will bury me
In thick cloth. Perhaps two husbands
Will be brought in and murdered.
One for a taste. One for the real thing to ask me
Not to come back from the underground. Do not expect me
To lie like an eggshell, not giving rise to anything.
I will crack the earth like a rice kernel, grow
Needles rolled in olive oil, wrapped in fifty-six winds.

*

No third marriage, photographer.

You will not take my light.

You will not take my hand.

THE HOLY GHOST

And fire rushed down upon their heads.
A common thought rushed down upon their heads—
to take a selfie
upon the sandbar splitting the sea;
to swim in their laces
as the tide rolled in, like a working stomach.
But can you call it a thought

when the herd thinks, *Move*,
a common tendency upon the air,
simmering on sand and grass,
in their very skin holding the wind; they
shift, almost
automatically—

And tidewater rushed down upon their heads.
They imagined themselves as glass vessels,
a hole in the crowns of their heads, a tunnel
through the palms of their feet—continuously
filled
with new water.

They thought to take a selfie on the beach
and opened their mouths, lit by their own flaming tongues.
And opened their potential for memory.
They thought to turn their faces, as one, to kinder light.
And glamour rushed down upon their heads.

And fiction rushed down upon their heads.

And a heat-seeking missile rushed down upon their heads.

A spot of red in the beak.

LATE, SEASONAL SHADOW

This new, cyst-like maturity—

Watching the sea, memory tagged in its cheek.

Its bulbous head and torso, pinched stem, robed.

The blade in its ear, an elongated blade—
it would cut out its lungs to breathe here

(the lungs needing to be seen)

A CATCH

This week I have carried my friend like
a personal sun at my shoulder:
right. Sometimes she purrs, sometimes lashes
out. Petal, forgive me, I have come
to you wretched and stunted. The
wooden band around my small finger
hexagonal, irregular, binds
me to you, I will not take it off.
We erode each other, give back each
other, dynamic as a circle's
time. I place my feet at the shoreline:

your feet are cold. Our hands loosen or
shrink, blood pulling us towards homeostasis.
The skin, interconnected, responds.
Like gulls in shift in an airflow, we
get there to where we are going, but
enough of this slow glass, help me with
branches to break it. Our skin, fragmented,
on shore, partly buried as sand blows
around it, diamond, fractured with
sunlight, a few warm patches at
our hands. Which ones shall we hold
            to cross this—

North;

South;

West;

East;

we form
the circle, watch
a gull crash
clam on the rock,
eat
the circle that will fuel
its body; another

flies closely by
with speed, yellow clam
in its beak—feeling what?
not the ocean swiftly
above it—and leverages
the speed to drop it,
crack it, lift its body in tendrils

with its black-spotted beak;
—   heralding of
waking, or peril?
Petal, the tumor.
Petal, the molecular crabs,
        working earthbound
        to follow a fallough.
Petal, the breast in this shell,
        the first /
        enemy / watch it.

BOUND TO THEM GILLS

In the guise of Aphrodite.
From the pastures of ocean,

which one of us emerges,
wig in hand and halo-headed,

slant foot forward like a knife in a
shark's belly, which one of us

praising—slick voice invisible /
in heaven, thing perceived murdered

into language spilt from a god's
throat who was sheep-headed,

Greek father, headache
tapped / tapping at the cock.

Father passing out gender like
skull lollipops.

As Athena. Apple in the sheep. Apple in the nigh, newly built
boat of genitalia sailing towards Hades, skimming the shoal-born
disturbance of being read; identified. Cloud-blinded eye in the mist
(Zeus)—through which this powerful woman will rise, sword-like.

REINCARNATION, WAITING FOR SOMEONE TO SPEAK

Petal is my gristle friend, the violet slash to my face

With her gristled wing joints, compensatory knife in her side,
crumpling, annoyed more than anything

To build the muscles back up in her back, she lifts her torn wings and
screams over the sink

A knife to pull from her throat, crisp against her teeth

A massive river behind that

A branch behind that

A chandelier behind that

A mind's blades

Petal is sifting through seawater, her twenty-six reflections

Patient, holder of time

Crosser-forth onto ocean with a mind of thicket

Director with an open sore mouth, blossom-lipped

Blue shield, eye at the fold of a branch against throat

Hurricane fire, language open fire

Star in the rib cage, sunk and delicate
as the folds of a dress underwater, fire under
blue wick

Slick metamorphosis in her bones, shaved, stilting on high feathers, her
hollow wrist

A plain from which she launches, shepherds in the distance, wanting a
shot of oxygen to the brain

Goes out, floodwater brushing the porch, her own hair unbrushed
Such men step to her

with their front teeth, wanting to nibble a little of her light

The taxidermist, the pastor, the carnival operator, the professor of
medieval texts

Men in their Lotuses, crossing over, their feathers on the ferry, real
debris

And and plastic, white footprints, laryngitital voices, the discontinued
spikes of their crowns

*

Petal divining a flesh will not be seen for days

With three sacks of bone and sand, three trees uprooted by hand,
woman raging on her knees, irradiation from her body blue-green,
chlorinated and loud

Dressed in skins she is crawling, moaning like a sheep, cradling selenite,
which hatches from its harbor of round edges two heads and a tongue,
a speaking across skins, sharing miracles

Her feet on the grass, her arms in the grass, a sudden, ecstatic union
with the torso she is laying in the way

Will you touch it with the wheels in your feet? Or leave it, going forth
from here, singing?

—When you are ready, Petal will take your hand, lead you to the place
she was born 1,002 years ago

As you enter the house her mother is dying in, the midwife is clearing
the table and laying Petal in a large shell with black cloth, a sacred seed,
a wing joint, a crown, a cup of rice, a cup of oil, a loudbranch

Before covering her mother with a shroud, cleaning the dishes, and
setting a meal for the dead at her feet

Her mother is lengthened daily as her muscles contract, so she is as tall
as she is when she is buried, four days later

While the loudbranch walks up and down stairs

While in a field nearby with constellations lighting up bright, though cold, two shepherds come to a shining dragon Her

glamorous neck and breasts Her

pink teeth and eyelight Her

tortured air, her mind resolving to silence

Their bodies prostrate to the ground
Do what you will,
they say, attached to God's will

And realize what they are listening to

And catch fire, hands heavy as snake-coils

Flooded in visions of light, transfixed, the ego in its little trick fills the
sky like weight, most unhelpful in the end

TO THE BENEFIT OF NO ONE

I Discover My Father Was Bullied in High School on the Suspicion that He Was Gay; I Discover My Father's Two Best Friends Were Gay and Perhaps He Did or Did Not Know It, Perhaps It Was or Was Not Difficult to Find Out; I Have Heard of One of the Friends, Whose Name Was Kenneth, from My Mother, Who Was His Friend, Who Watched Him Die of AIDS like an Orange Peel in a Hospital Bed, One Eye Kicked out of His Head; And Hadn't She Once Called Him to Me "<u>Our</u> Friend," Implying My Father; But I'd Imagined My Father a Reluctant Presence in the Hospital Room, Brought There by His Wife, Resentful of an Affiliation by Her Real Friendship with Kenny; What to Do Now with This New Picture: Of My Father Grieving over a Gay Man He'd Loved, Gathering Orange Peel in a Wastebasket with His Hands, Full of Veins?

Petal's father has failed her. She has a father. She has. Who has
failed to understand her making
even the possibility of being proud of her
void. Who feels she has
done wrong in being herself, wronged him, rot

in a low-down stump. Who feels carrying her sword
will scathe him. It will. Snake cut in half and the sword laid
between them, a barrier
mirror
of wants, their faces shown out of proportion, on their sides, light

laid in in metal. Beneath her is a body seeking approval.
Beneath him is a body seeking approval.
A family is not what you will
when you are lonely and loathed and oppressed. Do not tell her

to talk about it. Who has failed her, hands around the corpse's idea.

*

Who did get in her face, so close she could have
slashed him. And why didn't she.
His skin

a kinship she has raged against, his ease and settling a foil
terrace
she would rather jump off
than be his. Hands
overbright for her
branches. Hands shaking

in the stare-light of trauma.
She would rather live as this aluminum tree
than be his.

JIM AND EUGENE

The gander's cut neck. To stay together, loathing (the neck) with loathing (the body), to share a reason. Fit arms gnarled in the stow of filthy tarp and ax there in the pickup's deep cabin. Grey featherthing plastered in rain. A kitchen (Eugene's). A family (Eugene). A supper (the gander). A barrier mirror of wants (their utensils). A bright, distorted image before Jim, Eugene astride him. Two, Eugene's hands in his hair, his ear shining like gasoline sprayed on a garden. One, splayed to risk.

GUARD THE FATHER

HAVING BEEN BEHEADED IN THIS LIFE
BY MY FATHER WHO MISTOOK ME
FOR A LOVER

Rockwig is obsessed
with how gulls fly from here, four

and one apart; identifies
with the breast in rotation; slow tension
in the ligaments the way
bread tears.

With thought accumulated;
with his wing joints
in the loosened state that they are;
he will grain and grit as he carries his father

to the grave, hammer him in
with metallic singing
and fold his arms as is proper;
wrap the body

in tall grass, lay in with it
a thin ram.

ALL PARTS OF THE ANIMAL USED

—Rockwig:
Hornet crashing through the screen I have placed on my father, eyes
like a black and white pearl
for temperance. To hold water
over the river and pray—he will pass on with or without this, but I have
been taught this
recognition wherein someday, someone
will do this for me. I am in the process
of payment, his orange wings spread like an archer's. The rabbit-hearted
angels come to the bank for their hearts to be slit. There will be twenty
in addition to mine. He will be
sent off in the way according to the Godtext—twenty-one
hearts for his chest bones,
head of a sheep for his cock, onyx
in this third eye, to sleep.
Sister, Pupilslit, will take the knife
when I am done,
and carve the angel for luncheon,
hooves in the fire pit,
hooves in the community's glue.

*

—Sister, Pupilslit:

I am worried for my brother. He is a raving, epileptic bird with our father's death. I have caught him numerous times with a blade at his heart, moaning like a sheep, dressed in skins. He burns lime-green, in bed, covered in reams of fogged breath. I have heard him announce himself to death, broker an exchange in which flesh is penalty for mourning. Mornings, he takes off his grief and goes through a few hours himself, before, spotting a girl in the market or changing hands with a beggar outside, he stoops in his grief and I cannot see him. There are times I see only the small, white light of his crown flashing in the waves and want to pull him, like an entrail, out. I want him to live and suspect it is getting harder, surrounded as he is by false water. I really do not know what to do. Husband Papercreased says to let him pay, we do not know what he owes. Husband Starpedal has more sympathy, but then, they are very alike—two fires in a galaxy-lit desert, communing.

YOGA, FLESH IN A HOLE'S
CONSTELLATION

       —Pupilslit: I say to my husband, Papercreased,
Liar. I know what you do
with the sheep. They are gift wrappings
struggling against wind, thick paper
on the fence, and wet.

He will have none of my eyes, dark half
of his face to the sink. We are diseased
in this house as his nails, at night,
prowl after me with sheep's blood
and urine. We have been married for three years,

and to our husband, Starpedal, for two—who returned
to brood
and fuck and paint, battered blood
in his brain, thick and restless.
Breasts in shining water, pained breath

with his back in the mirror, whipped, chained,
stunning.
He comes for me and Papercreased, three
torched sounds in the area, the humans
hang ears at their doors.
Sink, flock, beat, trail, four
hands at my clitoris glitter, two necks
ache to a crown, a meat fit

to shellfire.
I am delicious and pertinent.

—Another ewe has given birth tonight, to a body
Papercreased has pulled from the branch being
too stupid to come out itself. His hands
cop a grasp in the slick. I will not be
compassionate,
as the ewe bleats like a dead star
and the lamb starts to work.

UNTITLED

Wind over nightwater—the light chills,
a constellation
stilting past the priest-trees into
a clearing, exposed, bullet meant
for its throat, onyx
crown slipped over its eyes, the entire
chakra of its body
stills. Ghost

thrown over the stag two angels
lift, and carry off.

To hold light in the blood.
To comb the hooves.
To take the limbs in your hands
and pull.

WEDDING DAY, GODLINESS

—And it was frightening to be adored,
contained in a similar idea
standing there, across from me, in my clothes
too muscularly, with a look
of too much kindness on my face.
I felt about it
a nuance—conflicting
aspiration, agitation, and fury, and a deep-seated
need
to kneel. There was fear involved:

of the foundation this was all being built upon, this
exaltation by one person or many;

of losing humility, my oldest value,
irregular, clear stone in the lawn;

I was *not* afraid
of disappointment.

*

Fatherangel flies out of his sockets, brandishing a switch-whip.
His eyes are tense molecules, seizing
the situation:
elk with a broken leg, boy angel with a club and bloody
wrists.
Fatherangel pulls the weight of himself against
little brother
like a mighty ship,
so he goes down, down for his sinning.
He is a pulp.
He is a paste.
He will not join in in the singing, as he has no lips
left.
He will be a sad penitent.
Inside his wing sockets, there haunt three living worms
that ache him in the middle of the night.

TOO COLD FOR SINGING

Small angels in the holly bush,
dim-witted but quick
for berries, single-pointed and warm.
They are sharing a word, bright
as God's knees. Force, force,
the blight it takes to crack
into a redflesh, juice splatter
at the neck and breast, thick-throated
with pulp. These days,
it is a green scrim
or a white scrim, both
rerunning with dark. Fatherangel
gathers in his hands for a feast:
the woken.

TANTRA

—Rockwig: At the infirmary,
I receive letters at U.S. Mail 3, lavender
set in the slant brick. I walk there. I am recovering
adequately, am walking and flying with support.
One of the nurses is shining on me, he

has a jealous friend. The two of them keep me company like
constant, covalent planets; at night, bringing me
alternative medicine, crush
sage into my wing joints,
oil my cock. We are young—there is little difference between healing
    and fucking, three
burning grounds in the intersecting distance. Papercreased

ties my wrists to the bedposts,
a mixture of permission and will,
his need at my throat
a high collar. I try to appeal more
than fear.
I hold my organs.

VESSELS FOR LIGHT STATIONED AT STRATEGIC POINTS

In the emptiness that follows reading,
comet, nailbird, Pupilslit
spreads over Rockwig like a chorus, her forested
heads and breasts.
Two bite into the light
of their orifices. Teeth at an armpit, import, impasse, teeth
at a wing joint of oil, the friction of which
lights it, and Pupilslit's back
burns
across the sixty-mile priest-woods. Priests turn up

to watch her, and shroud their bark
from falling skin;
track her progress
in the house of shared wealth, cinders
of spiritual progress.

*

—Rockwig:
When I close my eyes,
orange-blue suns like spots in paper
burn through. Fatherangel is behind
one of them. Fatherangel is behind one
of them. Fatherangel
is behind one of them with his veins
like a river and sixty
arms. I will wander, titanic,
through this tunnelbranch, pouring fire
from one bowl to another
as they burn up, and each bowl
is smaller.
What is the smallest light
you can see by?
—Think on it.
The priests call it *speed*

and pat the earth, a deepening
furrough from their centuries
of hands.

A CONTRIBUTION

Fatherangel readying the roast
as the cooking students input—
Exactly, one onion, cut-jupiter and the light
sheen through. Exactly, held
to the slick surface, and anguished.

But nasty, but despot,
the students murmur, casting forth their spirits
to turn nails in Fatherangel's wrists,
while their hands, outwardly, stay tucked
neatly, behind their mossy backs.

—What are they really learning?

Directions towards a politics, philosophy,
domestic life. Accountability
to a god who is sheep-headed, a mirror
in one eye, a shepherd in one eye, a blackrock
in one eye

that is taken out
and studied in times of crisis;
the elders gathering together
to commune on what they have seen
come to a negotiated conclusion; they

can make a lake out of an ocean.

THE NECK

All week I have passed it—
severed neck a stronghold for breeding.
I hear the neck buzz like a stitch.
Sometimes the tidewater shines on it.
Sometimes the tide is uncle-slack.
Or wholesale.
Sometimes the tide is like glue.
Sometimes tidewater transplants the sun
and the world has a permeable feeling.

THE BLOCK HORSE

Just me in my house-hooves,
        Petal, don't get so fancy.
Dream where you begged
        in the great hallway you
ate vanilla ice cream
        from a chalice in when
you first came to court
        with your uncle, a wise
man with moderate time
        for children,
King of Clubs, resting his head
        on his elbow. Petal, tiny
spoon to the rescue
        of the crushed bean-
people, a frivolous
        story you told to feel
kept, kept as a lapdog.
        I do not blame you if
you'd like to pause
        to remember the ice cream.
Perhaps you'd like to stand
        in this doorway in your
ragged robe and let the cold wind
        over your tongue.
You can pretend the fur
        of your arms is a worn
fur, fur of another
        animal, cast your howling

eyes away from your
        lot and stroke
your bad doll's hair, milky
        as slit apples.
Petal, how did you get so
        desperate, no silver
to your name, no silver even
        to buy the green candle you'd
need
        for this spell for money.
Make do, drawing
        the dollar sign into dust,
pull your sleeping mat

        over it. How luxurious
you have a sleeping mat. How
        luxurious you can wipe
dust from your floor, even if it is with
        your fingers. How luxurious
you have this stable with a
        door to the weather, purple
storm leaning in on the
        city. Here is a stone
to sleep with. Here is your
        uncle's first knuckle. The revolution
brews in the city's papered walls, soldiers
        bud in every corner,
fingernails painted with sunlight,
        starlight, lantern light in secret
meetings.
Be ready for their face at your door, adolescent,
        willing, a question framed

to your lips and the knuckle-stone
            containing its desert to be
thrown. They know
            of your power and want it, think
there is a bedful
            of money. Petal,

wasn't he wise, your uncle
            who taught you to read
and be still, block horse
            stationed in stall, stare ahead wanting
for nothing, whom
            you walked
the pasture in your pocket,
            like friends, bump of your
lips learning his language, rumble
            of his, showing it yours,
patiently, but firmly. You were
            a persistent machine, his
favorite
            arc of the sky
in your eyeball, a grey slate
            finance / marvel / shovel
with which whole lines of aristocracy were
            drug up. Just

my Joan of Arc screaming,
            nothing new, Petal-horse language
in my pit-bone.
What do we say? We say hymns, hymns.

HER CARRION WEIGHT

One of us is sick with heat, gold
light in her crown, overbearing.
A long haul

to the next town well,
with little water
we can share without

suffering. Very little
to be done, though we try,
give her a sponge

of vinegar to suck on.
We have heard, in odd ways,
this helps.

Her mouth, a pinched, dry sky.
Her mouth, the anus of a starfish.

The first group kneel down
to lift her.

ACKNOWLEDGMENTS

Gratitude to the editors of *Connotation Press: An Online Artifact, Glass: A Journal of Poetry, Glitter Tongue, High Chair, The Moments Collective, NILVX: A Book of Magic, Palette Poetry, Poetry Northwest, Prodigal, Tammy, White Whale Review, Winter Tangerine*, and Sibling Rivalry Press for anthologizing "Election Day" in *If You Can Hear This: Poems in Protest of an American Inauguration*. "The Tranny Ballet" and "Bound to Them Gills" first appeared in *Wig Heavier Than a Boot* (Kris Graves Projects, 2019).

Tarot: "This is a gift" is a line of dialogue from the film *The Craft* (1996). *The Five Shades in Her Neck:* "Tined and constellated" has Thylias Moss' Limited Fork Theory in mind. *A New Function*: "The world is bright" is a lyric from Barbra Streisand's "My Man," from the film *Funny Girl* (1968). *Made to Always Worship at One Station* was inspired by Gian Lorenzo Bernini's angel sculptures on view at the Harvard Art Museums. *Having Been Beheaded in This Life by My Father Who Mistook Me for a Lover* draws on the myth of Ganesha's beheading by Shiva.

Powerful energetic and practical support has been given to this book. Gratitude to my chosen family and family, to my mother, grandmother, sister, and father. Gratitude to my poetry teachers Mary Jo Bang, Carl Phillips, Kerri Webster, and Peter Cooley. Gratitude to Aaron Coleman, A.H. Jerriod Avant, Alec Hershman, Amanda Ackerman, Austin Segrest, Bhanu Kapil, David Johnson, Gabriel Kruis, Hilary Vaughn Dobel, Kristin Fleischmann Brewer, Justin Stott, Laura Neal, Leila Chatti, Maura Pellettieri, Sara Martin, and Sophia Starmack. To the communities of the Fine Arts Work Center in Provincetown, the Pulitzer Arts Foundation, and Wormfarm Institute. To Carey Salerno, Alyssa Neptune, Julia Bouwsma, and the team at Alice James Books.

Gratitude to the guides with whom I have made a contract. And to anyone who needs it now—this book is for you.

Neck of the Woods, Amy Woolard
Little Envelope of Earth Conditions, Cori A. Winrock
Aviva-No, Shimon Adaf, Translated by Yael Segalovitz
Half/Life: New & Selected Poems, Jeffrey Thomson
Odes to Lithium, Shira Erlichman
Here All Night, Jill McDonough
To the Wren: Collected & New Poems, Jane Mead
Angel Bones, Ilyse Kusnetz
Monsters I Have Been, Kenji C. Liu
Soft Science, Franny Choi
Bicycle in a Ransacked City: An Elegy, Andrés Cerpa
Anaphora, Kevin Goodan
Ghost, like a Place, Iain Haley Pollock
Isako Isako, Mia Ayumi Malhotra
Of Marriage, Nicole Cooley
The English Boat, Donald Revell
We, the Almighty Fires, Anna Rose Welch
DiVida, Monica A. Hand
pray me stay eager, Ellen Doré Watson
Some Say the Lark, Jennifer Chang
Calling a Wolf a Wolf, Kaveh Akbar
We're On: A June Jordan Reader, Edited by Christoph Keller and Jan
    Heller Levi
Daylily Called It a Dangerous Moment, Alessandra Lynch
Surgical Wing, Kristin Robertson
The Blessing of Dark Water, Elizabeth Lyons
Reaper, Jill McDonough
Madwoman, Shara McCallum
Contradictions in the Design, Matthew Olzmann
House of Water, Matthew Nienow

ALICE JAMES BOOKS is committed to publishing books that matter. The press was founded in 1973 in Boston, Massachusetts as a cooperative, wherein authors performed the day-to-day undertakings of the press. This element remains present today, as authors who publish with the press are invited to collaborate closely in the publication process of their work. AJB remains committed to its founders' original feminist mission, while expanding upon the scope to include all voices and poets who might otherwise go unheard. In keeping with its efforts to build equity and increase inclusivity in publishing and the literary arts, AJB seeks out poets whose writing possesses the range, depth, and ability to cultivate empathy in our world and to dynamically push against silence. The press was named for Alice James, sister to William and Henry, whose extraordinary gift for writing went unrecognized during her lifetime.

Designed by Alban Fischer

Printed by McNaughton & Gunn